BEING WITH GOD

Be Still and Know

Feeling at Home
In the Divine Presence

Michael J Spyker

AgapeDeum

Published in Adelaide, Australia by AgapeDeum
Contact: agapedeum.com

ISBN Paperback 978-0-64577720-3-6

Ebook 978-0-6457720-3-6

Copyright © Michael J Spyker 2023

All right reserved. Other than for the purpose and subject to the conditions prescribed under the *Copyright Act*, no part of this publication may be reproduced, stored in a retrieval system, or transmitted in any form or by any means, electronic, mechanical, photocopying, recording and otherwise, without prior permission of the publisher.

Publication assistance by Immortalise

Cover design: Ben Morton

Cover photo by Tomoko Ujion, Unsplash

Come to me, all who labour and are heavy laden.
And I will give you rest.
Take my yoke upon you, and learn from me;
For I am gentle and lowly in heart,
And you will find rest for your souls.
For my yoke is easy, and my burden is light.
Matthew 11:28-30

CONTENT

Chapter 1	A Vision	1
Chapter 2	Transformation	6
Chapter 3	In Spirit	9
Chapter 4	In Love	13
Chapter 5	Faith and Hope	16
Chapter 6	Faith	20
Chapter 7	Hope	24
Chapter 8	Undressed	27
Chapter 9	Be Still	30
Chapter 10	Peace	34
Chapter 11	Rugged	37
Chapter 12	In Abundance	41
Chapter 13	Freedom	45
Chapter 14	Just Living	49
Chapter 15	In Relation	53
Chapter 16	Foundational	57

1
A Vision

For as long as I have been a Christian, ever since I asked Jesus into my heart, I have felt at home with the Lord. Whatever the circumstances, whether I sensed it or not, I knew that the Lord was near. I have been in business, in ministry and an academic with all that involves and found living as a Christian uncomplicated in what mattered most. What did matter, could be a struggle at times, but a natural one. Much of it involved the questions personhood is commonly faced with.

I hold that a successful Christian life is foremost determined by what kind of person I am rather than by my 'spirituality'. I commune with Jesus in my spirit often and he helps in me mature. My studies, with an emphasis on spiritual theology, I have enjoyed. I have desired understanding and will keep on seeking it. All quite satisfying with the Lord guiding me and giving insights. Always, the Lord is readily found by those who wholeheartedly seek him.

Much has been written about being with God. It is hardly possible to present new ideas. And yet, I am writing another book about it. It is prompted by a vision the Lord gave not long ago. Allow me to tell you what happened. I cannot escape the feeling that this present little book needs writing as a response. There is nothing new under the Son, but at times some truths can do with a little dusting off to have them shine more brightly. Reading them afresh may sharpen the spirit and enliven the heart. In troubled times to come, as suggested in my vision, that will be helpful.

***

A Vision
When sick with influenza in 2022 God gave me a vision. What I saw came to me distinctly. What it meant I didn't know. I mentioned it to a few friends without getting much response and let it be.

Certainly, it was a vision and not a dream or hallucination. Ignatius Loyola, founder of the Jesuits, taught his monks to never trust a divine communication of significance unless it came instantly and out of nowhere. It had to be unrelated to anything the mind was busy with. It happened to me in that way. With a feverish head I suddenly saw something extraordinary. I might have been terrified, but wasn't. The Lord was my protector.

It was like sitting in the movies close to the screen for a short clip with powerful intent. From a deep darkness a bright index finger was coming my way. It was red, yellow and black, obviously infected and with a sharply pointed filthy nail. When it was up close, I detected a shadowy face full of menace with a revolting glee. It exuded the ability of doing incredible evil as it pleased and was taking great pleasure from that. Intuitively, I understood that the face was no threat to me. I felt revulsion on being confronted with this spiritual power. The thought of Jesus on the cross shot through my mind.

The vision changed. I saw the feverish finger move slowly, full of stealth and wickedness, up along the back of a person. Next, it rounded its shoulder and was aiming for the heart. Furiously I twice shouted, 'You bastard!' A last evil grin and the vision ended. I found myself back with the discomforts of the flue having no idea why all this was happening to me.

***

Only once before, now decades ago, have I had a vision.

Briefly, the Lord lifted the veil on the magnitude of God's love. It totally floored me. Ever since, that incredible love towards creation has been foundational to my understanding of personhood and God's divine plan. My books testify of it. However, I knew this second vision was not meant for me alone. Its scope was broader and I let it rest, waiting for understanding.

I began to feel the need to 'do something' with that vision of evil. Obviously, the Lord would not have given it to be left in the too hard basket. It dawned on me that the vision meant exactly what it so clearly showed. It is a serious warning: Beware! Danger ahead! Evil is creeping up from behind! I understood that the vision's purpose was to activate a response.

The present state of the world gives the feeling that something unforeseen may be ahead. Matters are fragile and global strife is increasingly raising its head. Wars and rumours of wars every day. Unstable financial systems and unprecedented weather. Just to mention a few of the present upheavals. Forecasters of doom are aplenty. The Church belongs to this world and is facing the same future. It seems the heavens are shaking and the Lord is warning of challenging times ahead.

The vision, I believe, is a call from the Lord to his people encouraging an increased focus on Him, who is an ever present help in trouble. It is not a call to spiritual warfare. The power I saw would simply deflect any such attempts and is solely for the Lord to deal with. Not the Devil needs attending to as an enemy, but Jesus as a Friend. *Being with God* is all about the latter; about what I have found to matter most in that regard. In many ways it is nothing new, for Gospel truths are not complex and readily known. But then, reading up on them afresh with possibly a few ideas that you may not have thought about, can only be positive. The topics to follow are not usually part of a modern discussion on spirituality that mostly concerns the esoteric. Such insights are worthy of attention, though I consider the key to being with God in accordance with the nature of Jesus less 'spiritual'. Prayer is important, of course. Meditative reflection I engage in all the time. However, it is good living where the Lord is my helper 24/7.

2

Transformation

Most of my life has been taken up with 'ordinary' living that has been transformed in the presence of the Lord. I have found keeping my eye on the ordinary quite essential in support of the 'spiritual'. By ordinary I mean decent, good living. It is what the Lord expects of every person on earth and as such is nothing special. I must put my best foot forward here. Without living out the 'ordinary' proficiently I cannot mature as a Christian. A simple truth that highlights the fact that the 'religious' aspects of Christian living are not the most important.

What I am like as an everyday person needs constant attention. As does the disposition of my soul. Apostle Paul expressed his desperation in finding tendencies within himself that prevented the life he had in mind. Inclinations that tried to drag him down even though his desire was towards the good only. Paul concluded that though he could not change this situation, he would make the best of it. Jesus would not hold his shortcomings against him. One day the power of sin, which Paul earmarked as being the problem, would disappear forever and he looked forward to that day (Rom. 7: 7-25).

Paul's struggles will resonate with everyone who is of good will. Often in his letters to the churches he addressed behaviours that were troublesome. Put away anger, wrath, malice and slander, and foul talk and don't lie, he commanded. Instead, put on then compassion, kindness, lowliness, meekness and patience. Forgive each other and put on love (Col. 3:12-14 & 5-7)). None of this can be classified as 'religious'. 'Put on the new nature,' Paul exhorts, 'which is being renewed in knowledge after the image of its creator' (Col. 3:10). That new nature involves the formation of my soul. Soul is what I experience because spirit and body interact. It is my everyday awareness and shows what is happening within me, both the good and what is questionable.

Heralding in 'the new' is the primary theme in Paul's understanding of the Lord and the Gospel. It sums up what the death and resurrection of Jesus has made possible, so eloquently expressed in Paul's exultation: 'I am a New Creation!' A brand new person I now am, Paul declared. Not merely as a nice religious idea, but as a powerful reality that is active. This reality is birthed into every Christian and must be nurtured into full maturity with the help of the Holy Spirit. Behold, the old has gone and the new has come! I must tap into 'the new' every day by involving the Lord in all my doings. It influences my personhood at many levels, those I have control over and deeper levels where I have not. Progressively the nature of Christ develops within me. Nothing perfect, but good enough.

The nature of the Lord within me is not 'spiritual' in the usual understanding of that word and yet very spiritual indeed. It is the ordinary in me becoming supra-ordinary. The aim of Christian living is lifting the ordinary into spiritual significance, e.g. the fruit of the Spirit. Diffusing some of its fragrance every day is important. As a student of spirituality I have never felt 'spiritual'. Sure, there have been spiritual moments and may it continue. Finding intimacy with the Lord however is for 'ordinary' people who wholeheartedly seek him. The Lord takes great pleasure in well lived ordinary lives. When the ordinary becomes transformed and is infused with something new.

3
In Spirit

Apostle Paul exhorts to 'seek the things that are above, where Christ is seated at the right hand of God. Set your minds on the things that are above, not on things that are on earth (Col. 3:1-2). Advice which Christian history shows to be frequently not adhered to. The things that are above become translated into the rules of dogma that are below. The ways of God may become perverted and politicised. Through the ages much blood has been shed in the name of the Lord. Wars and persecutions have been many. Recently, the Russian Orthodox Church blessed Putin and his war effort in Ukraine. All of this while Christ is seated above in a place of Love. Understanding what God is like is an age-old problem.

When Jesus met the woman at the well in Samaria, she raised the question of what would be the right place at which to worship. Would it be Mount Gerizim, where she worshiped, or the Temple Mount in Jerusalem? Jesus responded by telling her that God is spirit, not bound by place and time nor religious tradition (John 4: 7ff). The magnitude of God mostly defies human understanding. Any rationalisation of divine reality will only scratch the surface, while intuitive perception ever partly senses what God's nature is about. Only Jesus fully knows his Father and helped in revealing some of it. A revealing that continues for the believer privately through a Person to person encounter in the Holy Spirit. God looks for those who will worship in spirit and in truth, Jesus told the Samaritan woman. Not at which 'mountain' it occurs. When directly engaging with God in spirit, religious preferences and rituals will fall away.

Set your mind on the things that are above, Apostle Paul wrote. Those things involve God's nature and plan for creation. I must keep both in mind every day for it shapes life for the better. God's nature translates into good and caring living, while faith in the divine plan raises me above the mundane. I know that God is with me and one day will make all things well. Furthermore, when Jesus spoke of worshiping in spirit and in truth, he had a specific truth in mind: that I be true and honest before him, hiding nothing. When being lifted up into the realm of God simply being human is all that counts. Being open before the Lord is a liberating experience.

While on earth Jesus, had difficulty in explaining the nature of God for Jewish religious tradition had obscured it for centuries. The idea that God is love, and how much so, his listeners didn't quite grasp. That God is not distant but readily found was hard to comprehend. Christians readily accept these ideas but they can remain just that – ideas. When they sparingly enter affective experience and the sense of them remains at the level of intellectual consent. When the notion of God remains enveloped in rites, rituals and particular preferences which signify the things that are above but only sometimes penetrate them.

Gerizim or Temple Mount, the Samaritan woman asked Jesus? Something quite different, he said. You must worship God in spirit and in truth. Anywhere will do, but it needs to be a spiritual engagement, a personal interaction. Talking about God is very different from talking to God. Doing for God is good, but it will not come close to being with God.

God transcends the world and I am invited into that reality. A mode of greater being is there to be discovered; a way of living that steps up from the ordinary. It moves out of the 'religious' and into the divinely 'relational'. It is that worship the Lord is looking for and every believer is capable of it. In a fragile and uncertain world I do best in taking it seriously.

Jesus says, 'Come!' 'Come to me, all who labour and are heavy laden, and I will give you rest' (Mat. 11:28). In my spirit I may simply come, nothing more complicated than opening my heart to him and believing he is intimately present. 'Behold I stand at the door and knock,' the Lord says. He is easily found, always invites and will never demand. 'If any one hears my voice and opens the door, I will come to him and eat with him (her), and he (they) with me' (Rev. 3:20). I take pleasure in reaching for the things that are from above, every day.

4

In Love

Being in love with the Lord is a blessing. It is a state of being more than a feeling, a certain knowing of being divinely well cared for. That realisation sustains me daily. God's love powers the universe, is ever present and seeks to connect. All I have to do is reach out for it in my spirit and try to live out the nature of Christ. In this my intentions and efforts matter more than continued success. The Lord understands and is kind.

How kind is well described by Lady Julian of Norwich (1342 –c 1423) in one of her visions. 'And I saw that he is to us everything which is good and comforting for our help. He is our clothing, for he is that love which wraps and enfolds us, embraces us and guides us, surrounds us for his love, which is so tender that he may never desert us' (Showings, chapter 6). It is this love that the Lord offers freely to every person. I am conscious of it and this awareness sustains me.

Jesus came to demonstrate the love of God. It is what his mission was all about. Insights from the mystics in Christian history speak of detecting a wondrous love. In fact, seers of all major religions agree that fundamentally all is based on love. Creation is an act of divine love and finds its functioning in that power. Sin arrived as the spoiler and somehow infiltrated the very fabric of creation from the beginning. We will never know how that became possible; why God allowed it. That mystery is to remain hidden.

The love of Jesus is out of this world, literally so. Made in the image of God, I may have a sufficient sense of it however to figure what Lady Julian is talking about. Although the measure of Jesus' love is beyond me, I am able to meaningfully interact with it in my spirit. I am being loved but the depth of that love will remain a mystery. Why I am thus loved is clear. Because, God *is* Love. Everyone and everything is divinely loved, for the nature of God cannot do otherwise.

Being loved brings a sense of belonging. I may feel at home in the divine presence. Belonging is the bedrock of relational security and without it life feels adrift. By faith I enter my belonging with the Lord finding comfort in his embrace. This reality is of significance to the wellbeing of my soul. Life can be lived without it, but never quite in the same way. Somehow, I sense the constant care of the Lord, rain or shine. I am divinely loved and in that knowledge face what life brings to me. In turn, I know the importance of offering belonging to family, friends and colleagues. The principles of love that derive from the Trinity need expressing into everyday life. Allowing people a place of care and respect is an essential.

People are in need of love and good living spreads it about. It is what God intends for humanity. In ethics the golden rule holds that you treat others the way you want to be treated yourself. As Jesus said: 'Love your neighbour as yourself.' This is the second commandment. The first one is pertinent in finding intimacy with the Lord. I must love God with all my heart, soul, mind and strength (Mat. 22:37-39). It sums up the Christian life in a nutshell.

    The kind of life Jesus invites me into is a challenge. I need to overcome the influences of sin within me as best I can with the help of the Holy Spirit. It is reasonable of God to expect the right attitude and behaviour of me towards people and nature, while the invitation to love God wholeheartedly, I gladly accept. The love of the Lord spurs my motivation and heals my soul.

5

Faith and Hope

The importance of love is readily understood. When not being loved by someone life withers. Harry Harlow's famous but cruel experiment with young monkeys being deprived of motherly care has proven it. The little ones were miserable and though properly fed, lost weight. Love nurtures into wellbeing while its absence causes disintegration.

Love, as a reality in creation, originates with God. When Apostle Paul writes about Christians presently seeing in a mirror dimly with regard to the essence of God, he enthuses that one day all will be clear. I will fully understand and know myself to be fully understood. He then makes the comment that although whatever is involved in human endeavour with regard to God will fall away, faith, hope and love will remain, with the greatest of these being love (1Cor. 13:8-13). That love remains is obvious for God *is* love. But how about faith and hope?

Faith and Hope

References to faith, hope and love often appear at the beginning in Paul's letters. 'Because we have heard of your faith in Christ Jesus and of the love which you have for all the saints, because of the hope laid up for you in heaven' (Col. 1:4). Paul writes about, 'your work of faith and labour of love and steadfastness of hope in our Lord Jesus Christ' (1 Thess. 1:3). Love, faith and hope are central to Paul's theology. They remain eternally, in God's eyes are worthy of lasting value, and as such unique. What might have made Paul so convinced of this? I'm not sure, but let's consider it. Obviously, it is important.

Without faith it is impossible to be a Christian. Faith is the facilitator in making God known. People are capable of faith as is shown in the many religious expressions found in human history. Without believing in them, the gods become meaningless. People need love and also the expressing of faith, something to believe in that connects the heavens and the earth. Somehow, the security of the soul is at stake, that sense of being part of a universe rather than merely an apprehensive sojourner on the face of the earth. In our modern days of self-sufficiency this need for faith has become less acute, and yet, the search for some kind of spirituality remains widespread.

Apostle Paul understood that when faith wavers, the foundations of a belief in God become unsettled. Faith, like love, is an ability that must remain positively activated. I have an innate sense of faith within me and it must translate into expression. Doubts that will arise, need to be waylaid by what Scripture tells me about God and the divine plan. Any faith involving a spiritual belief engages with mystery. To me, an incredible God shrouded in large mysteries is an exciting proposition. Mysteries that have been partly revealed. The narrative of who God is and what it is all about make sense and presents a wonderful reality. On that knowledge my faith rests and it is sufficient.

Hope also has eternal significance. Apostle Paul pointed to an eternal future that one day will come to an incredible fruition. Already now, by faith, I may engage with it. Hope looks forward to it in anticipation and offers something to hold on to. When Paul writes of hope in our Lord Jesus Christ, it involves both future and present. A future place has been secured for me in God's house, while presently Jesus is certain to guide me every day. Hope involves the unseen and most of God's doings remain undetected. Only by faith will I know the Lord to be active, always.

Love, faith and hope are foundational to Christian living. I must keep their awareness alive within me as it furthers the wellbeing of my soul. What makes faith, hope and love especially significant is their remaining eternally. The import of that I don't know but to say that their presence in my life helps me cope better. Let's discuss it a little further.

6

Faith

Early one morning I reflected on how to approach a certain long-term task. I thought about faith and how that might help me along. Was I in need of a gift of faith perhaps, mentioned by Apostle Paul (1 Cor. 12:9)? I didn't think so. The 'claim it and frame it' idea came to mind, but it never much appealed to me. Ever since becoming a Christian I have practised faith for the need of it was made clear early in my walk. Situations urged me to start talking to God seriously. My prayers were answered, often over time and in subtle ways that only later became obvious. Sometimes there was no answer or perhaps it escaped me. But I know my life to have been divinely guided in consistent and hidden ways. God is faithful, always. Faith is essential in being a Christian. Everything about God becomes real through faith.

Scripture describes having faith as firmly believing with certainty. 'Faith is the assurance of things hoped for, the conviction of things not seen' (Hebrews 11:1). As an example the writer of Hebrews mentions that God created the material universe out of nothing. A rational person can only accept this as a certainty by faith.

A not uncommon approach in facing difficulties, or having desires, is using faith and an expression of power. The thought that I will make things happen in the name of the Lord. When having this conviction while praying over people it can be harmful. A negative outcome then sometimes is attributed to a lack of faith, particularly that of the prayer recipient. The egocentricity in this method is troubling. Fortunately, many declarations of faith do not involve over-confident egos and so much good is achieved. Not for a moment would I suggest giving up on expectantly believing before God.

In reflecting on my task ahead that particular morning I sensed that another way in using faith was possible. It suddenly dawned on me that I could 'walk into faith'. I could walk with my problem into faith and affirm every day in my mind that the Lord is actively involved in shaping a solution. The idea was a little startling but it appealed. Walking into faith is somewhat different in that it is not a striving or an act of spiritual power. Instead of an energised prayer activity, it is a resting in trust. Walking into faith is relationally focused. It is intimate and enjoys a secure dependency before the Lord.

I move into this 'relational' faith simply by remaining in touch with Jesus. It is not my power but his that makes all the difference. By faith I focus on the certainty that the Lord is ever present and active. Whatever bothers me, whatever wisdom is sought, I mention it in prayerful reflection. If an idea comes to mind that is relevant and feels right in my spirit, I thank the Lord and walk it into faith. I will keep on walking while finding ways in which to make the idea happen. Perhaps the Lord may do the unexpected, though usually it remains steady as she goes with the occasional lapse of conviction to be rebuked in my spirit. I am far from perfect at this, but it's a great way in which to keep my faith vibrant.

The idea is far from startlingly new, but it has a good feel about it. Whatever comes my way, I walk it with the Lord into faith. Every day, that faith lingers unobtrusively in the background of my awareness. Quite unlike resorting to faith only when a problem arises. Intimacy with Jesus creates a day and night faith reality. Sometimes assertive declarations of faith in the name of the Lord may well be appropriate. There is power in the Holy Name. Usually though, I simply remind the Lord of his promises in reflective prayer. The Lord never needs convincing of what he is known to be about and I may take heart from that. I must be confident before him in the knowledge that his ways are higher than mine and may differ from the expected at times. I will walk the walk of faith right into eternity.

7
Hope

Love, faith and hope will remain. Hope is the third eternal quality of significance. Hope involves the future yet to come and belongs to everyone's reality. For Christians that reality, and their hope, is extended by a heavenly future. It brings a different perspective into life, more so when this hope becomes a daily awareness.

Hope is the desire for something to happen with an expectation that it could. Outcomes are never sure, which makes hope such an uncertain emotion. The only certain hope on offer involves the promises of God, who is able to fulfil those without fail. Thus Christian hope can be such a positive in an unpredictable world. Apostle Paul speaks of the hope in our Lord Jesus Christ. That hope offers me promises and facts, like having been born again. For this reality to become alive in me it needs the support of faith, which is 'the assurance of things hoped for, the conviction of things not seen (Hebrews 11:1). Christian hope is faith based. They are two sides of the same coin.

Hope is a difficult emotion to deal with. It can linger within the psyche relentlessly with potentially dire outcomes for wellbeing. 'Hope deferred makes the heart sick,' Proverbs states (13:12). People may hang in there against all hope to their detriment, but not give up. Hope tends to hold on until there is closure. Our world can be a terrible place. There is no avoiding that and I find refuge in the presence of the Lord. Not as an escape, but as a way of managing being alive. Within me resides Christ, the hope of glory (Col. 1:27).

Hope involves believing in what cannot be seen nor controlled. Spiritual realities fit that bill. Much about the Lord is invisible and bound to remain so. Faith convinces me of what Scripture presents as truth. Like that the Holy Spirit is my helper and Jesus will see me through (Heb.13:5-6). I need never be alone in what befalls me. With great care the Lord controls my present and my future. These are powerful spiritual certainties bringing proper outcomes, even though I will not always have a real sense of it.

Christian hope brings a distinct perspective into life. While not insensitive to the sufferings of the world, which are horrible to say the least, I may hold onto the hope of its eternal future: when God will make all things well. I may find rest for my spirit regardless of the strife, in a world that surely also offers many a beautiful thing. When calamity strikes, I will seek to remain steadfast in faith remaining close to the Lord in a certain hope that he is active on my behalf. When a situation becomes truly hopeless, I must resign myself to that experience. The Lord will carry me in my grief. Finding myself curled up in a foetal position because of hurt is tough. Taking that hurt into the hurt of the cross elicits a feeling that is hard to describe. It offers an understanding of the Lord unlike any other and strangely brings some healing. Not ever will I question whether God has departed me for divine love never will. I have no answer to suffering beyond that one day it will end and by God's command be translated into glory.

Hope can be tenacious. Some people keep on hoping against all odds. It is what Christian hope should be like, unwavering in its convictions. Made easier because much of what is hoped for is a certainty in God and simply needs to become alive by faith. My hope has one eye on situational circumstances and the other of heavenly promises. Christians will suffer like anyone else, but God has placed the comfort of hope in their hearts. When I hope gratefully, the shackles of being overly bound to earthly realities fall off. Jesus came to set me free.

8

Undressed

In the Genesis story Adam and Eve lost their freedom and apprehension entered their lives. After taking a bite from that lethal apple they felt naked, disassociated from God and hid behind a tree. When God called out, 'Where are you?' they were vulnerable and afraid. It is ever God's question to humanity. God clothed Adam and Eve so that divine glory would not consume them. Dressed in animal skins that hid their nakedness they were to face their new circumstances. It is the situation of people today. Their souls remain covered up against the glory of God, while a hostile world forces them to clothe their egos with a protective façade.

The sacrifice of Jesus on Calvary has changed human potential. I may come away into the open from behind that tree, which God now sees as a cross. Availing myself of resurrection truths, I may step out into God's glory without fear. I am invited to discard the clothes that cover my soul and approach the Lord naked in spirit. My façade should fall away.

Such a step is challenging and can be easily avoided. Christians may face God with their ego still mostly dressed, which the Lord accepts. But it will restrict their becoming intimate with him and limits possibilities of spiritual maturity and its advantages. A liberation from deep fears and insecurities will remain incomplete, while the divine present is not enjoyed as it could. With the soul partly in hiding, potential in Christ is hampered. My relationship with the Lord will lack the necessary depth.

Our modern world likes to overcome the shame of being naked by defiantly showing that naked is fine. Privacy is to be challenged. Not before God though against whom an extra layer of soul protection is considered expedient. While it is with God that undressing the soul is safely possible allowing entrance into the pleasures of divine love. Where the true self finds assurance of being fully known and accepted. What more would I want?

Society has conditioned me in being on the defensive to the point that shedding the clothes of my inner being before the Lord seems a daunting proposition. Fully unwrapping the existential protection of personhood takes a bit of doing. Superficial prayer is always an option but hurts in the soul will not thus become fully healed. Only unreserved intimacy with Jesus will achieve that over time.

At its best the Christian life is courageous. It dares to have faith and hope in what cannot be seen. It approaches the Lord with heart and soul. In the Song of Solomon the woman who loves her prince ends up realising that, 'I am my beloved's and his desire is for me' (7:10). True love commits all, spirit, soul and body.

Transparency and honesty are central in having a close relationship with Jesus. 'Just as I am,' is key. With nothing hidden, my release from idiosyncrasies, illusions and disappointments begins. The Lord will shine a light on the struggles of my inner being and knows the way forward. He will guide over time ever leading towards improved psycho-spiritual health. It is a process that has its challenges. Occasionally, what the Lord asks may be painful but is for my own good. No longer will my soul be dressed up protectively against the glory of God. The cross has made that glory my wholeness.

9
Be Still

Scripture tells the story of Jesus sleeping in the boat while his disciples fought a storm that could have them all drowning. Finally they took courage and woke Jesus up asking whether he didn't care that they would perish. Jesus said to the sea, 'Peace! Be Still!' The wind ceased and there was a great calm. The Lord then asked his disciples why they had been afraid; didn't they have any faith? They wondered who this Jesus really was, that even the weather obeyed him (Mark 4:7-40).

In expecting his disciples to have faith and be unafraid while in such peril, Jesus was asking too much, it seems. He was not suggesting they could have stilled the storm, but that they should not have lost heart. Everyone faces difficult situations in life, sometimes seriously so. When God says, 'Be Still', invariably it involves troublesome circumstances in which holding onto faith is necessary.

An example is found in Psalm 46 with the writer

reflecting on serious strife between the nations. Those 'nations may rage, but the Lord of hosts is with us,' the psalmist concludes (46:6-7). The beginning of the Psalm declares God to be a refuge and strength in times of trouble. It concludes with the well-known verse: 'Be still, and know that I am God' (46:10).

Nobody likes trouble, but invariably it will arrive. I then have a choice to make. How much do I believe God to be in control? Will I hope against hope, or hope in expectation? The latter is what Scripture is advising no matter what things may look like. It is not easy to keep a vibrant spirit when negativity presses upon it. The thought may come to mind that I am fooling myself when trusting all to come out okay. It may seem that matters will remain unresolved. When the wild waves were crashing into the disciple's boat, it sinking looked far more likely than getting safely ashore.

Jesus said, 'Be Still!' to the elements of nature and they obeyed. Perhaps he simultaneously spoke into the psychology of his disciples urging them to calm down. They saw a miracle solve their problem. Not so in situations where Christians may be left wondering about the effectiveness of their prayers. They do well in remembering what the Lord told Thomas: 'You have seen.

Blessed are those who have not seen and believed' (John 20:29). The Lord is always active and mostly unseen.

Hanging in there with God can be difficult. The prophet Elijah learned all about it. He was exhausted and felt he had failed God in the task set for him. The Lord guided Elijah away from his circumstances to be refreshed. He ended up in a cave in the desert all alone. After a while, Elijah was told to go stand on a hill before this dwelling. Scripture explains that a manifestation of God would pass by Elijah. A massive storm soon drove the prophet back inside the cave. The storm was followed by an earthquake and a fire. But the Lord was not in any of these powerful forces and finally appeared as a still small voice that brought Elijah once again into the open. After all the turmoil, he found God speaking to him quietly and with great love. Elijah was told how to carry on with his life (1Kings 19:9-15).

Sugar-coating the Christian life with promises of riches, happiness and health is imprudent. The Lord isn't against these when wisely administered, but it never occupies the forefront of his mind. Far more important to him is the question: 'Do they trust me unconditionally, always?' Life can be unpredictable for believers and unbelievers alike.

Positives and negatives happen to both. In hard times a trusting in the Lord outweighs wealth and health in its effectiveness. It is those times that Jesus helps me grow.

Taking to heart the directive of 'Be Still' settles the spirit. Worldly troubles can easily engulf and are beyond me solving them. Personal situations may threaten to overwhelm. Those are the times in which my spirit must reach into the divine realm of the Lord and find its refuge simply by being quietly before him. Not in a shut-up kind of way, but in partnership with the Holy Spirit and fully engaged with what God sees fit to happen. 'I can do all things in him who strengthens me' (Phil. 4:13). Whatever situations may look like, God is a very present help in trouble (Psalm 46:1).

10
Peace

When Jesus told the storm to be still, he prefaced it with the shout: 'Peace!' In Aramaic he would have used the word 'Shalom!' and not per chance for it is one of the most important concepts in biblical history. It features in significant moments like when Jesus presented himself to his disciples for the first time after his resurrection. 'Shalom be with you,' he said twice, and followed it with, 'As the Father has sent me, even so I send you' (John 20:19-21). As a Christian I must be a bearer of shalom.

The Aaronic benediction ends with, 'The Lord lifts up his countenance upon you, and give you peace (Num. 6:26). This idea of peace as expressed in the concept of shalom encapsulates the vision God has for humanity and creation. Walter Brueggemann in his book, *Living toward a Vision*, writes: 'The vision of wholeness, which is the supreme will of the biblical God, is the outgrowth of a covenant of *shalom* (see Ezekiel 34:25), in which persons are bound not only to God but to one another in a caring, sharing, rejoicing community with none to make them afraid.' The wellbeing of nature is much included in this intent of God.

Blessed are those who offer shalom for they are close to God relationally and will reveal the divine nature best (Matt. 5:9). Intimacy with the Lord means buying into the vision of shalom, engaging with what in essence God is about. The nature of God is not religious but relational – an expression of love and care in all that is required. Shalom is a vision of harmony within all of creation in which 'the wolf shall dwell with the lamb ……. and a little child shall lead them' (Isaiah 6:8). It is our eternal future.

This vision, that originates from divine reality, I will only partly taste of while on earth. But seeking that taste is important. In life, whatever I find wholesome, I consider it to involve shalom. There is no point in analysing this notion too much. The concept of shalom is beyond being pinned down by neat formulations. It is far too dynamic. Brueggemann writes that, '*Shalom* is not subject to our best knowledge or our cleverest gimmicks. It comes only through the costly way of caring.'

The degree to which I am a shalom person is determined not by how spiritual I am, but by the disposition of my soul – how much I seek the wellbeing of the other.

This applies to everyone. It is quite possible that a non-believer expresses the vision of shalom better than an egocentric Christian. Those who offer shalom, whether knowingly or not, will receive shalom within their psyche. It is how personhood works, by God's design.

'Peace is just a word, it's just a word,' Annie Lennox sings in desperation. The way our world is travelling that seems true enough. In the history of humanity the Shalom of God is hard to find. And yet, it is always active in some way and eternally is a certainty. When intimate with the Lord shalom invariably occurs, for he *is* our shalom (Eph. 2:14). Always, when something rocks my boat, (like with the disciples in that storm) Jesus will settle my soul. Shalom is not merely a worthy philosophical idea, it is a divine vision that is active and encompasses all. I will do well in living toward this vision with love, faith and hope.

11
Rugged

Some moments in my walk with God I will always remember. In my early days as a Christian I was facing a situation that got me a bit riled. My emotions had a hard time. But the Lord told me 'no rebellion'. It was not a demand for submission. A God, who is love, never does submission. It was an invitation to agreement, as all God's instructions are. I learned a valuable lesson that day and have never since rebelled against situations that came my way. Objected at times, for a while, but never without agreeing to live through my situation with as little complaint as possible. A few times I failed initially and it harmed my wellbeing. One can but learn.

A life close to the Lord has a ruggedness about it. It is robust and never shuns times that can be rough. Every noteworthy writer in the history of Christian spirituality testifies to that. The wealth and health Gospel with its many pitfalls for the ego is a misrepresentation of what matters to God. The 'thou art a serious sinner' message can suggest submission and likewise is a perversion of the real thing. Yes, I am living under the power of sin. However, God understands and has come to the rescue. The Lord seeks to lift me into a new way of living in which sin still is pestering, but I can have the upper-hand in Jesus (Rom. 7:21-25).

In Christ, I have become a partaker of a good news that invites towards my formation in accordance with the nature of God. I can take it or leave it – be a mediocre Christian, or one who accepts that sanctification can be a rugged road. Not in any sense an impossible one for the Lord is my helper. But often it will ask the best of me and potentially to the level of some suffering. Apostle Paul advised to rejoice in suffering for it builds character which results in a hope that does not disappoint (Rom. 5:3-5). Instead of the word rejoicing I would suggest the idea of remaining positive. In difficult times one of the first words I remember is, 'no rebellion'; just ride this wave as best you can. Occasionally, waves may arrive that will dump and crush. Then 'no rebellion' will sound harsh and yet it remains the best way forward with time as a healer. Meekness can be a struggle.

The thought that people don't like the idea of character has been disproven by Davis Brooks' book *The*

Road to Character that became a US best seller. It seemed to touch a need. Many folk feel to be insufficiently equipped in facing the world around them. Psychology has come to value the necessity of character in gaining wellbeing as well. Anyone close to Jesus will know that without the shaping of character, the best of God will remain in abeyance.

'No rebellion', the Lord said to me. He might well have added: 'Put your hand to the plough and toil the soil I will guide you toward. You are invited to become the farmer of your own soul and grow it into maturity. You will pull up the weeds diligently and nurture the tares. Not merely by your own strength, but with the help of my Holy Spirit. The rain will come and the sun will shine. Storms will seek to subdue you. But with rugged persistence, at times at the cost of your desires and with suffering, you will bear significant fruit; much to my pleasure and that of your own. Consider the cedars of Lebanon.'

Life dishes up all sorts. Fine people go through painful circumstances. There is neither rhyme nor reason to it from a human point of view. The ravages of sin in the fabric of creation are many. The Lord offers little insight apart from telling Lady Julian of Norwich in one of her visions that, 'Sin is necessary.' Jesus came to undo its power at great cost on a rugged cross. He secured a fabulous future for creation, which a believer in him may enter already now.

The Lord came to defeat the power of sin and liberate people from its clutches. That liberation must bear fruit within the souls of those who love him. Christians are invited to be courageous and none are more so than those taking on the defects of their own nature in the desire to become more like Jesus. Willing to commit to this challenge with dogged persistence is what most pleases the Lord. Such a believer is convinced that Jesus is close, always. They feel at home in the Divine Presence

12

In Abundance

The Lord does not give of his Spirit in half measures. However, living under the influences of sin dulls the sense of the treasure I have within. About wellbeing, the Lord explained in the story of the Good Shepherd that, 'the thief comes only to steal and kill and destroy; I came that they may have life, and have it abundantly' (John 10). His comments were made in reference to Jewish religious history and how it had failed its people in representing God. Jesus, by the sacrifice of himself, would open the door to a new way of living.

That way has arrived and is now a spiritual reality. But the thief is still active in snatching at its possibilities. The frailty of human nature remains vulnerable to its defects with harmful consequences. Being egocentric, full of pride and unteachable, offers no benefits that are good for the soul. These tendencies and other questionable ones are common in what people are about. They are though detrimental to the abundance of life that the Lord has on offer.

Abundance means that what is needed is readily available. God, who owns the cattle on a thousand hills, is well able to provide. Some Christians strike it rich and there is nothing sinful about wealth properly managed. While others may have to live sparingly in accordance with divine providence. I have no wisdom regarding that. The first though doesn't guarantee God's abundant living, while the second is not cut off from it. Having life, and having it abundantly, mostly concerns spiritual wellbeing. It is the spiritual that taps into the abundance of God.

Early on in the parable, Jesus explains that when the Good Shepherd has brought all his sheep out of the sheepfold, 'he goes before them, and the sheep follow him, for they know his voice.' Further on Jesus declares: 'I am the Good Shepherd; I know my own and my own know me.' This statement holds the key to the abundance of life available to every Christian.

So, what might this promise of abundant life be like? That question cannot be answered definitively; a few observations must suffice. Success in finding abundance is much determined by my relationship with the Lord. 'My own know me,' Jesus said. Four words with great potential. 'I know my own,' he declared also. How much I know the Lord depends on my willingness to open my soul before him and let his light shine in. Knowing the Lord is reciprocal. The more I allow him to reveal myself to me, the better will I understand him. Such a revealing is always kind and not accusatory. 'Come,' Jesus said, 'I am gentle and lowly in heart' (Mat. 11:29).

With most of my days now behind me I must say that life has been abundant. Many experiences, challenges and good times have come my way. Difficult times also, but even those have their benefits in learning how to find some rest for the soul. Not easy, but being able to fall back on Jesus' presence has been a blessing. When one day heaven awaits, I feel to have lived okay, nothing perfect and all by the grace of God. Simply, because I have tried to come and 'know him.'

Abundant living is a treasure to be opened. This treasure has divine significance and spiritual power. The world is looking for something akin to it as is shown by the popularity of self-help books, including those about kinds of spirituality. Christians are privileged in being invited into a special spirituality of abundance. But will the Lord's voice be heard; a voice that only sensitive, spiritual hearing will detect? The abundance of life on offer by Jesus originates from deeper than what a solely natural life has available. My spirit has been enlarged with a divine blessing. There is great benefit in following the Good Shepherd.

13

Freedom

Once I came across an interesting observation about freedom that reads: 'Freedom means not that you can do as you like, but that you can become what you should.' It is good advice. I suggest the Christian idea of freedom to involve three aspects. Firstly, there is situational freedom, demands that derive from my circumstances. For instance in Australia, when driving on the left side of the road responsibly, I am free to traverse the whole continent. Secondly, there is a liberation of the self to aspire to. Negative emotions like anger bind up rather than set free. And lastly, there is the freedom in Christ that opens my spirit to the promises of God. In all three the Lord is active. I know him to have protected me on the road travelling Australia wide. Surely he has enlarged my soul and his promises are my delight.

Regularly, Jesus was at loggerheads with the religious authority of his day. At one point he went as far as to say that though thinking themselves free spiritually they had the Devil as their father. Only 'if the Son makes you free, you will be free indeed' (John 8:36). He told some Jews that believed in him, 'If you continue in my word, you are truly my disciples, and you will know the truth and the truth will make you free' (John 8:31-32). They took umbrage believing that as the descendants of Abraham they had never been in bondage to anyone.

Accept what Jesus says about himself, live out what he stands for, and that is real freedom. A freedom that involves the depth of personhood. It liberates into feeling fully oneself, not constantly pestered by doubts and negativities with the ability to navigate life in a psycho-spiritually healthy fashion. It is quite something and only possible when close to the Lord.

Jesus told the Jews, 'I am the light of the world; he who follows me will not walk in darkness, but will have the light of life' (John 8:12). In that light I will find my freedom, when it illuminates the path ahead and obstacles to overcome. The question I often ask myself is, 'how much freedom do I have when walking around within my soul?' Are there matters I have not dealt with that need attending to? Those may be as practical as apologising for a mistake or as deep-seated as a grudge. When the light of life is allowed to shine into the corners of my psyche, it will reveal the infections of my soul that need healing. For instance, with anger I know it to involve an unfulfilled desire in the belief that I have been short-changed. The way to deal with it is to tell myself that 'it's okay' and not hold it against anyone. In facing situational difficulties I will try to accept the circumstances for what they are without complaint – no rebellion! In all of this the Lord helps and in that way I maintain my freedom. Sometimes, I sit before him with trouble in my soul and ask what is going on. I may be given an insight, or possibly not. If the latter, I continue my day in the knowledge that in due time my inner freedom will return.

An important aspect of maintaining the freedom of soul is forgiveness. Jesus insisted knowing how damaging not doing so can be to wellbeing. Once I have forgiven someone I must keep on reminding myself that the person is forgiven and must suppress old hurts that may seek to bubble up. Also, I will do well in forgiving myself for mistakes made. My inner freedom depends on it. Not that I will ever forget the big ones, but they must be just a remembrance that may still embarrass. It keeps me humble.

Psalm 23 is everyone's favourite and for good reason. It describes the 'freedom of being' people are looking for. It declares the Lord to be my Shepherd; the one who says that someone who is free in him, is free indeed. That freedom is a gift to be entered into and developed within personhood. It is a divine gift to those who take the Lord seriously. They may avail themselves of insights that are life changing and bring wellbeing. Being with God lights up my life, silences what is unhelpful in my soul, and makes known the way forward into true liberty.

14

Just Living

Thomas Merton, famous monk and author, later in life and after many years of teaching spirituality, began to wonder about its adequacy. Contemplative experiences with the Lord he valued. Undoubtedly, he treasured the insights given to him over many years. In the end, in spite of that, Thomas concluded that his way forward was 'to just live.' Of course, that living was guided spiritually and subconsciously by all he had learned. 'I just live', was an expression of letting go.

With 'just living' there is a difference between knowledge and really knowing. Knowledge fills my head space while actual knowing is a deeper process. Such knowing may be because of factual information gathered, reflected on and digested to the point of it being internalised. It may happen that I know intuitively by sensing the value of certain ideas without much consideration at all. All my intuitive knowing will have Scripture as a safeguard; my understanding needs to measure up.

The reflections in *Being with God* are meant in support of 'just living' the Lord's way. Their value is in heightening the awareness of who I 'really' am in Christ. This understanding needs constant attending to. It must remain fresh in mind and spirit. At times the Lord may challenge me to live a certain insight out. Mostly though I spend time with him in a 'just nice' fashion, enjoying his presence.

Much is determined by the disposition of the soul – its spontaneous behaviour based on personality and lived experience. My disposition is what the Lord will focus on in helping me grow. When Thomas Merton concluded, 'I just live', it was with a Christ-like nature that was years in the making; from the moment he had accepted the Lord's invitation to come and learn from him.

Generally, the idea of 'I just live' is what people do much of the time. Merton, in a sense, was falling back on what he had always been doing. What he was inferring was that he would be more relaxed about it, not so focused on spiritual pursuits. There is wisdom in that for the Lord said: 'My yoke is easy and my burden is light' (Matt. 11:30) Jesus cares and is not a hard taskmaster. A.W. Tozer observes that, 'God is easy to live with.' Aspiring to the nature of Christ is an objective that must be approached in a balanced way. I have learned that the humbler I am, the easier it is to get the balance right. The disposition of my soul is formed by what life brings plus the influences of the Lord. Also, by what I have read and studied.

The Lord is pleasant to be with. Walking on earth he was a holy man who played with children, mixed with the poor and dined at the tables of the important. If not for his message and miracles, he would have been seen as an interesting but ordinary man who is kind and good company. Nothing about him smacked of importance and superiority.

Christians, who are close to the Lord, likewise are congenial while expressing the fruit of the Spirit. They are not prone to favouritism and contrived behaviour. Their interests are held without chips on shoulders while their demeanour is a willingness to listen to different points of view with a possible modification of their own. They are deeply Christian, but do not come across as such unless feeling so guided. Simply, they just live.

Their conscience and promptings are influenced by the Holy Spirit, which to themselves usually seems rather ordinary. God moves divinely in natural ways. When something important needs to be conveyed, the Lord has ways in putting that across. In the writing of my books I know to be guided, but it might seem that all is my own inspiration.

Years ago, I heard a preacher say Christians are supernaturally natural. I like that idea. Natural, just like anyone else, but supernatural due to divine influences. When Thomas Merton decided on, 'I just live', it is seems ordinary but of course it is not. Just living the Christian way needs cultivating. It requires continual stimulation through prayerful reflection and also reading up on what being a Christian is about. Life is a large canvas with many challenges. Jesus offers rest for my soul and encourages me to relax. Rome wasn't built in one day, nor is my maturity. Most of the time, 'I just live'.

15

In Relation

Over the years, I have regularly written about relationality. Everything exists in relation, as also the sciences and philosophy recognise. The dynamics of relating are relevant to the whole of creation and particularly so to personhood with its moral capacity. Get relating right and much will fall into place for the better. None of this is surprising for creation exists and holds together in a God who *is* love, the ultimate in relational expression. We live in a relational universe.

Decades ago I made a study of relational dynamics in the Trinity and discovered three primary principles that define the interactions of the three Persons. The first one, obviously, is Love. It is the nature of God. The second is Authority, whereby the role of each Person is defined. And the third is Unity for though a threesome, the Persons are One God. As God will not create but in accordance of the divine nature and functionality, it follows that those three principles are embedded into creation and are of particular importance to the human being, who exists in the image of God.

My little book *Living Well – the Art of Making the Best of It* presents a relational model based on Trinitarian principles in a non-religious manner. It includes insights on Place-making, highlighting the importance of helping others to truly belong. The Trinitarian Model recognises *love/care* and *authority/responsibility* plus *unity/integrity* as essential to positive relating. The seven steps of behaviour for each principle offer a psycho-spiritual outcome. For *Love* that outcome is the ability to *Love* in turn. Benevolent *Authority* leads to bringing a sense of *Freedom* to a recipient, while the principle of *Unity* brings *Wholeness* to the soul. In personhood negative relational dynamics are active as well due to the influences of sin. Their outcomes are *Rebellion*, *Anarchy* and *Weakness* of the psyche.

The model has guided me in understanding how to best fulfil my relational duties and what to avoid at all cost. I am briefly mentioning these insights to show that how God relates can be expressed on earth and is relevant to its wellbeing. Not only that of people but likewise of nature. With the Lord not being 'spiritual', the positive relational intent of any person counts heavier before him than pious or religion-based behaviour. When religion relates in accordance with the Trinitarian principles, it gains the Lord's approval. Anything other, and it becomes questionable.

In seeking intimacy with the Lord my behavioural expressions every day are first to be kept an eye on. I will make mistakes, but must aim for what is good. Most troubles in the world are relational in origin, when the negative has the upper hand. That applies to interpersonal relating as well as societal issues. Wars occur because of dictatorial behaviour that is *Oppressive*; that will *Neglect* the wellbeing of others and *Manipulates* into submission by its propaganda. These are the three behavioural principles deriving from sinful tendencies. With strife of a lesser kind than war the same relational negatives are in play, as is the case with troubles at an interpersonal level. It may be expedient for parties to separate, but usually it happens because people dig in and positive relational outcomes are considered to be unattainable.

This brief exposé hopes to convince that getting relating right is important. It is an expression of God's nature and open to all. Every person has a God given spirit and from that spirit relating issues. The Trinitarian principles can be expressed by innate ability and when anyone so does, the Lord will appreciated it. People are relational, for better or worse. Continually, they relate to themselves also. Self-talk is a determinant in wellbeing and the positive and negative principles apply.

Much of what the Lord will seek to remedy in my soul concerns the relational. My relational imprint needs healing for, as life is, I have been hurt. My relational intentions need sharpening, bit by bit. How I function relationally is of interest to the Lord and ever on the agenda. He never points the finger and always encourages toward betterment. Our Lord is positively relational to the core. So am I, and knowingly so.

16

Foundational

Jesus' story about building a house on a rock for it to withstand the test of time is well-known (Matt. 7:24). A solid foundation is essential to a building if troubles are to be avoided. I like architecture and in my spare time have done some building, loving the manual effort and creativity of design. My last project was to finish renovating a 100+ years old country church into a home. It was a beautiful little building with 9 stained glass windows, a timber interior, painted stone walls and a mezzanine floor with king-sized bed. The vestry had become a bathroom. Just gorgeous.

Old buildings often lack sufficient foundations. The little church was just okay, but cracks in the walls were happening. Also, it suffered from salt damp, as often is the case with old stonework. When foundations sag it is possible to pump and expanding foam underneath that lifts the walls and closes the cracks. That wasn't quite necessary with our church.

Inside the atmosphere was special, more so when the sun was shining through the stained glass. However, on dull days a few skylights would have brightened up the interior. We no longer own that little church due to family circumstances. But it is nice to know that instead of deteriorating the church, with its new outbuildings and landscaping, should stand for another 100 years.

This story figuratively reflects the Christian life. Jesus is both the rock of ages and the light of the world. When cracks appear, then the foundation of my spirit needs underpinning. I must let the light shine in also. The skylight in my life affirms that though being firmly anchored in earthly reality, heaven is my future. My circumstances are temporary and part of God's eternal plan. It is the only way in which I can make sense of the world.

Psalm 46 opens with the declaration that, 'God is our refuge and strength, a very present help in trouble.' Verse 4 states that, 'There is a river whose streams make glad the city of God, the holy habitation of the Most High.' When nations rage and kingdoms totter, the Lord of hosts is with us, the psalmist writes; a statement relevant to our world's current predicament. From a Christian perspective that river of God may be the Holy Spirit. Christians are its temple and can rejoice accordingly regardless of circumstance (1Cor. 6:19).

I may tap into that empowerment. Not by psyching myself up into faith, but with a confidence that derives from knowing that all is in the open and well between myself and the Lord. The cracks in my soul are known and will close up over time. My spirit may bask in the light of God, while my mind will never forget that I am participating in a divine 'project' that is yet unfolding and finds itself at a difficult stage. The end result has been secured, but as yet remains a hope that is anchored in the faith of conviction. All will be well – eventually.

Philippians 4: 4-7 is well-known, when Apostle Paul writes those lines: 'Rejoice in the Lord always; again I say Rejoice.' It is followed by an exhortation to pray and ends declaring, 'And the peace of God, which passes all understanding, will keep your hearts and your minds in Christ Jesus.' The word rejoice infers 'being quietly confident.' That Paul uses the word twice shows its importance to Christian living.

If my life is built without attending properly to its foundation and cracks are showing without reparation, then when the storms of life begin to hit, that sense of being quietly confident will become problematic. My spirit has not been trained for it. Furthermore, when not used to taking a heavenly perspective into daily life, it will be difficult for me to see the calm behind the storm. The five wise virgins kept oil in their lamps, always. The five foolish ones neglected it to their detriment (Mat. 25:1-13). Life is greatly enriched with the Holy Spirit burning brightly. For that to happen time must be set aside to be with God who is always immediately present.

The Lord works in miraculous ways. This little book focuses mostly on the inner person for that is where, in partnership with the Holy Spirit, my strength resides. Many a time I have heard of how God intervened in believers' circumstances, from a house being spared from fire, miracles of healing, and so forth. It is wonderful. Presently, there is much talk about the Lord coming back but that has been so throughout Christian history. Only the Father knows the day and the hour, and that must be sufficient. The best I can do is to keep the oil in my lamp burning with a steady flame – a calm spirit.

Psalm 46:10 reads 'Be still and know that I am God.' The vision the Lord gave me of that filthy hot finger indicates trouble. The right response, whatever may be the difficulties, will be to seek intimacy with the Lord. Life offers the good and the bad and there is no escaping it. The good lifts the spirit. It is the bad that discourages and makes life hard. In both the Lord is near. It is just for me to find him. The Good Shepherd never sleeps and I am welcome to feel at home in his presence.

AgapeDeum

Other books by Michael J Spyker

Walking with God
What are the essential pieces of the puzzle called 'God' and how will a concise explanation of their importance read? What will the full picture look like? *(Also free e-book)*

Meeting Emma
An introduction to Christian Spirituality in which Emma learns from theologian Joe how to involve God's spirit in everyday living.

Drawings and Reflections
52 short reflections on Christian vibrancy with full-colour illustrations by Jeanne Spyker Hardy.

Julian's Windows
A contemporary love story that contextualises many teachings of medieval mystic Lady Julian of Norwich.

The Language of Love
A love story that encourages wisdom and wellbeing, and seeking an authentic relationship with Jesus Christ.

Science and Spirit
How science and spirit exist is relation and what that means to Christian understanding.

The Primacy of Love
How a theological understanding that creation is essentially an expression of God's love leads to a model that explains the dynamics of human relating based on the Trinity.

Oh My Soul!
The meaning of soul, the roots of its awareness, and how soul health is helped by a Christian understanding of the dynamics involved.

Living Well
The art of making the best of life relationally. Though based on Christian insights this little book is meant for everyone and avoids religious references.

I Am Willing
A story about miracles and more based on the ministry of Dean Knight, who authors this little book with the help of Michael Spyker.

Shalomat
An adventure in which two young people are being chased across Australia while seeking to fulfil a riddle that has global consequences. The story is based on ideas from spirituality and philosophy.

Available at agapedeum.com

www.ingramcontent.com/pod-product-compliance
Lightning Source LLC
Chambersburg PA
CBHW072021290426
44109CB00018B/2301